Social Media

 Connect with a community of *Bible Studies for Life* users. Post responses to questions, share teaching ideas, and link to great blog content. ***Facebook.com/BibleStudiesForLife***

 Get instant updates about new articles, giveaways, and more. **@BibleMeetsLife**

The App

Simple and straightforward, this elegantly designed iPhone app gives you all the content of the Small Group Member Book—plus a whole lot more—right at your fingertips. Available in the iTunes App Store; search **"Bible Studies for Life."**

Blog

At ***BibleStudiesForLife.com/blog*** you will find all the magazine articles we mention in this study guide and music downloads provided by LifeWay Worship. Plus, leaders and group members alike will benefit from the blog posts written for people in every life stage—singles, parents, boomers, and senior adults—as well as media clips, connections between our study topics, current events, and much more.

Resilient Faith: Standing Strong in the Midst of Suffering
Bible Studies for Life: Small Group Member Book

© 2014 LifeWay Press

ISBN: 978-1-4300-2899-4

Item: 005602638

Dewey Decimal Classification Number: 234.2

Subject Heading: Faith \ BIBLE N.T. 1 PETER—STUDY \ PERSECUTION

Eric Geiger
Vice President, Church Resources

Ronnie Floyd
General Editor

David Francis
Managing Editor

Gena Rogers
Sam O'Neal
Content Editors

Philip Nation
Director, Adult Ministry Publishing

Faith Whatley
Director, Adult Ministry

Send questions/comments to: Content Editor, *Bible Studies for Life: Adults*, One LifeWay Plaza, Nashville, TN 37234-0175; or make comments on the Web at *www.BibleStudiesforLife.com*

Printed in the United States of America

For ordering or inquiries, visit www.lifeway.com; write LifeWay Small Groups; One LifeWay Plaza; Nashville, TN 37234-0152; or call toll free (800) 458-2772.

All Scripture quotations, unless otherwise indicated, are taken from the Holman Christian Standard Bible®, copyright 1999, 2000, 2002, 2003, 2009 by Holman Bible Publishers. Used by permission.

Bible Studies for Life: Adults often lists websites that may be helpful to our readers. Our staff verifies each site's usefulness and appropriateness prior to publication. However, website content changes quickly so we encourage you to approach all websites with caution. Make sure sites are still appropriate before sharing them with students, friends, and family.

Life can be tough. We need a resilient faith.

How would you describe your faith?

Faith may come easy to you, or you may be like so many who struggle with trust. For all of us, when difficulties knock on our door, that faith is tested. And for some of us, our faith is shaken.

How can we maintain a faith in God that is resilient, a faith that—no matter what happens—withstands the ups and downs of life?

In this study, we will look at the Book of 1 Peter, a short letter that shows us what resilient faith looks like. Mark Twain said, "Faith is believing what you know ain't so." This study from 1 Peter will show, however, that Twain's idea of faith "just ain't so." In fact, a resilient faith grounded in Christ is quite the opposite.

We will discover that resilient faith:

▶ provides an actual foundation for a sure hope for mankind.

▶ frees you to do what is good and right.

▶ helps you find joy even in a world of pain and suffering.

▶ is yours because of the sure resurrection of Jesus Christ.

It's good to know that, because of Jesus, a strong faith—a resilient faith—can be ours. We can stand strong regardless of what comes at us.

Mary Jo Sharp

Mary Jo Sharp is an assistant professor of apologetics at Houston Baptist University in Texas and is the founder of Confident Christianity apologetics ministry. She is a former atheist from the Pacific Northwest who began to doubt her faith in God several years after becoming a Christian. Her search for answers to her doubts about God led her into the field of apologetics. She is the author of *Why Do You Believe That? A Faith Conversation*.

contents

SESSION 1

FOCUSED FAITH

What situations tend to rattle you?

QUESTION #1

#BSFLfocused

Our faith is focused on a sure hope.

THE BIBLE MEETS LIFE

"I hope the weather changes." "I hope my team wins!"

As a society, we typically use the word "hope" in the sense of wishing for something to happen (or not to happen). We've transformed hope into something cold and temporary—something unreliable—because we've connected it to a combination of luck and human skill.

This view of hope is dangerous for those of us who follow Christ. Why? Because the way we think about hope influences the way we think about faith. It's our ability to hope for something better and bigger than our current situation that enables us to act in faith.

Thankfully, there is Someone we can trust even in the darkest of times—Someone who will never leave us hopeless. We don't have to settle for anything cold and temporary; we have a living hope!

In the Book of 1 Peter, the author doesn't just tell us about hope; he tells us about the foundation of a sure hope. And that kind of hope is the focus of a resilient faith.

WHAT DOES THE BIBLE SAY?

1 Peter 1:3-9,13 (HCSB)

3 Praise the God and Father of our Lord Jesus Christ. According to His great mercy, He has given us a new birth into a living hope through the resurrection of Jesus Christ from the dead

4 and into an inheritance that is imperishable, uncorrupted, and unfading, kept in heaven for you.

5 You are being protected by God's power through faith for a salvation that is ready to be revealed in the last time.

6 You rejoice in this, though now for a short time you have had to struggle in various trials

7 so that the genuineness of your faith—more valuable than gold, which perishes though refined by fire—may result in praise, glory, and honor at the revelation of Jesus Christ.

8 You love Him, though you have not seen Him. And though not seeing Him now, you believe in Him and rejoice with inexpressible and glorious joy,

9 because you are receiving the goal of your faith, the salvation of your souls.

13 Therefore, with your minds ready for action, be serious and set your hope completely on the grace to be brought to you at the revelation of Jesus Christ.

Key Words

Living hope (v. 3)—Expecting with certainty the resources to face life's difficulties and the encouragement that comes when life is hard because of the resurrection of Jesus Christ.

Revelation (v. 7)—Disclosure of what has been hidden. Though presently with His people, Jesus is not seen, but at His second coming, He will be revealed physically.

Hope (v. 13)—Peter used hope in much the same way Paul used "faith": as trust in God for the future. It is the certainty God is working, not mere wishful thinking.

1 Peter 1:3-4

Peter opened his letter with a greeting of encouragement. He used the imagery of birth—of new life coming into the world—to imply that once we've trusted in Jesus for salvation, we're like newborn children. We've only begun our journey, and much will happen on the road to becoming a mature Christian.

We have also been born into a living hope. This is a great encouragement for those of us who experience doubt, fear, or suffering. The hope established through Jesus' resurrection is a sure and certain hope, not something that depends on our circumstances or moods. That's because the guarantee of our hope is based on who Jesus is and what He has done.

Jesus' resurrection defeated not only the main consequence of evil—which is death—but also all evil in general. His death and resurrection provide a guarantee that all evil will be overcome and judged. Since Jesus isn't just any man, but also God, this defeat is final and binding. It cannot be overruled, changed, or taken away. The hope provided by the resurrection of Jesus is that good actually does prevail in the end. There is something better to come: the restoration of goodness.

Because our world can be full of trials and suffering, we sometimes despair or lose confidence in God's presence and work in our lives. But Peter pointed out that our inheritance through Jesus is a certainty that cannot be taken away when times are hard. It's a solid truth that withstands even the heaviest of storms. Since we can have confidence in Christ's victory over death, we can certainly have assurance of His power over every kind of pain or sorrow. This, then, is our firm anchor in times of trouble—a mighty foundation indeed for hope.

> *In what ways do human expressions of hope compare to the inheritance described in verse 4?*
>
> QUESTION **#2**

1 Peter 1:5-7

Peter declared that believers are protected by God's power. Maybe you're wondering: *If that's true, then why didn't He stop _____ from happening?*

God's protection and power can be a sensitive issue for those who've suffered or grieved over difficult circumstances. It's true that His protection may include your physical circumstances, but it also goes far beyond that to the spiritual realm of your faith (v. 7). Remember: your physical body is not the whole "you." You are also a soul.

Modern culture bombards us with a naturalistic view of the world that focuses only on the material. Consequently, we can fall prey to thinking that if God doesn't save us from physical suffering or death, He isn't saving us at all. We forget that the person who is "you" resides in the spiritual realm as well. Peter reminds us to focus on our salvation in Christ—the result of faith—rather than on the current suffering in the body. In this life, it's our genuine faith that endures.

We tend to look to faith as a last resort when all else fails. This is backward! Faith should come first. It's the driving force of life. Faith is grounded in the sure hope of resurrection. The physical part of us may fail, but our hope isn't based on protection from the physical ills of this life. Our hope is grounded in the resurrection of Jesus Christ, which points us toward eternity.

So why am I suffering? We may not understand our suffering now, but we'll find clarity with the appearance of Jesus at the end of time. We'll see the beauty of our trust in God that withstood the evils of this world. For now, though, the trials we experience in this life show the genuineness of our faith. And the genuineness of our faith will result—as Peter pointed out in verse 7—in praise, glory, and honor at the revelation of Jesus Christ.

> *How have you seen faith tested and strengthened because of a trial?*
>
> QUESTION #3

> *How have you experienced the connection between faith and joy?*

QUESTION **#4**

1 Peter 1:8-9,13

When we greatly love someone, we go "above and beyond" to express that love. That certainly describes the way God has expressed His love to us, and it can be mirrored in our own love as Christians. Christians have a love that originates from the One who created us and everything else. This love is unfailing, pours out in great joy to others, and extends beyond the limits of this life.

Such radically faithful love can appear foreign in a world that too often experiences disappointment more than faithfulness. How do we show the truth of an unfailing love to such a world? The answer is that our love for God—and how we display that love to others—is tied to our trust in Him.

As we face daily problems and wade through struggles, our actions and attitudes must be informed by the trust we have in our future hope—the sure confidence that things will get better, either in this life or the life to come. Granted, such trust isn't always easy. That's why we must make a conscious decision to improve in our own trust of God.

How do we improve in that way? Begin by trusting God in the small things. If you don't start there, you won't trust Him in the big things.

In verse 13, Peter called us to do two things:

1. Be sober-minded and serious, with our minds in a state of readiness.

2. Set our hope in the salvation that comes through faith in Jesus' resurrection.

When we begin to understand our hope as something real and grounded in the reality of the resurrection, we should see a change in the focus of our daily activities and lifelong goals. Everything we do should point back to the reality of the sure hope we have in our resurrection at the end of time.

> *How can our group reflect hope in a fallen world?*

QUESTION **#5**

WHAT DIFFERENCE DOES IT MAKE?

Choose two.	Record how hope in Christ can influence your perspective on these elements of life.
☐ My health	
☐ My relationships	
☐ My finances	
☐ My work	
☐ My future	

"Our future hope is not simply a theological doctrine with little or no practical application. It is, in fact, an ethical hope. It has behavioral consequences."

—THOMAS D. LEA

LIVE IT OUT

How can we respond to the reality of a sure hope?

▶ **Trust in the small things.** Seek out situations in which you can consciously and intentionally express your trust in God each day.

▶ **Prepare your mind.** Move your focus beyond the material world by reading a book or listening to a sermon series that solidifies your understanding of basic Christian doctrines.

▶ **Proclaim the gospel.** When you encounter someone who has lost hope, choose to share the good news of Jesus' resurrection and your sure hope for eternal life with Him.

Walking in the sure hope of Christ won't help the weather get better or spur your favorite team to victory. But it will give you a foundation on which you can stand and say, "I may get rattled, but I won't be moved. So bring it on!"

The Calm in the Storm

In typical Monday-morning style, with a coffee stain on my favorite pair of khakis and a Toy Story band-aid covering the shaving cut on my ankle, I took a deep breath when we finally got in the car about 7:30. Strapping on my seatbelt and backing out of the driveway, Sam was complaining about my musical selection when I saw blue flashing lights in my rearview mirror. In disbelief I pulled over, approximately 400 yards from my front door. Another Monday had begun, and peace was the farthest thought from my mind.

To continue reading "The Calm in the Storm" from *HomeLife* magazine, visit *BibleStudiesforLife.com/articles*.

My group's prayer requests

....

....

....

....

....

....

....

....

....

....

My thoughts

SESSION 2

ACTIVE FAITH

What are some things the average person considers holy or sacred?

QUESTION #1

#BSFLactive

Live a life that is set apart for God.

THE BIBLE MEETS LIFE

You're in a crowded room and suddenly everyone turns to look at you. Under the weight of those stares, your heart starts racing. Maybe a bead of sweat breaks out on your brow, and you take a half step back, looking for a way to hide within the wallpaper.

If you've ever felt that way, you're not alone. Most Americans— 61 percent—would rather blend into the crowd than stand out.[1] This tendency is so strong that fashion designers and advertising moguls bank millions on our desire to look and be like everybody else.

For followers of Jesus, the problem with our habit of blending in is that the Bible calls us to be set apart. In fact, the Scriptures command us to think and behave differently than the world around us. This has nothing to do with fashion or branding; it has everything to do with lifestyle and character. We are called to be holy—to be set apart— because Jesus is holy.

As we'll see in this session, the Book of 1 Peter helps us discover the joy of living a life that is set apart for God.

WHAT DOES THE BIBLE SAY?

1 Peter 1:14-19, 22-25 (HCSB)

14 As obedient children, do not be conformed to the desires of your former ignorance.

15 But as the One who called you is holy, you also are to be holy in all your conduct;

16 for it is written, Be holy, because I am holy.

17 And if you address as Father the One who judges impartially based on each one's work, you are to conduct yourselves in fear during the time of your temporary residence.

18 For you know that you were redeemed from your empty way of life inherited from the fathers, not with perishable things like silver or gold,

19 but with the precious blood of Christ, like that of a lamb without defect or blemish.

22 By obedience to the truth, having purified yourselves for sincere love of the brothers, love one another earnestly from a pure heart,

23 since you have been born again—not of perishable seed but of imperishable—through the living and enduring word of God.

24 For "All flesh is like grass, and all its glory like a flower of the grass. The grass withers, and the flower falls,

25 but the word of the Lord endures forever." And this is the word that was preached as the gospel to you.

Key Words

Holy (v. 15)—Separated or set apart for God. By nature, God is distinct, different, set apart, holy. Similarly, believers are to live distinctly, too.

Fear (v. 17)—Not terror but reverent awe or proper respect toward God in light of the responsibility to live holy and to live consciously of God's judgment.

Word of the Lord (v. 25)—The gospel or good news that God uses to bring people new life that His people are to proclaim.

> *What is your reaction to the commands in verses 15-16?*

QUESTION *#2*

1 Peter 1:14-16

It seems a little odd to me that in a letter written to a group of persecuted Christians, Peter threw in a reminder to be holy. Pain and suffering can have a way of leading us to God, but they also can steer us away from God. It all depends on our individual response. Some people will try to do what is right, no matter what it costs. Others will do whatever is easiest to handle a difficult situation.

We need the reminder to live holy lives. There have been many times where I handled a situation in a way that reflects my selfishness rather than Christ's holiness. My background is that of a do-it-yourselfer, an overachiever, and a naturalist. So when faced with a huge problem, I want to revert back to my old ways:

1. I don't see the spiritual side of things; I just see the problem. (That's the naturalist in me.)

2. I obsess over the right way to handle the issue. (That's the overachiever in me.)

3. I try to fix whatever I can on my own without getting help, since getting help will take too long and involve possibly messy relationships. (That's the do-it-yourselfer in me.)

To live by the truth is to live a life set apart for God—a holy life. Peter reminded us not to slip back into our former lifestyles and habits, but to continue to pursue what is good and true. He reminded us to pursue Jesus even through times of great trial.

In verse 14, Peter encouraged us to live as obedient children. In my experience, children are labeled as "obedient" when they trust their parents even though their instinct is to rebel.

On the other hand, the rebellious children I've seen over the years are the ones who scream and throw fits to get their way. Sadly, Christians can be exactly like those rebellious children when we handle situations with out-of-control feelings and self-centered goals. Instead, we are called to face problems with an intention of striving toward holiness—because the One we profess as Lord of our lives is holy.

WHAT IS HOLINESS?

Which of these images best illustrates your understanding of holiness? Explain.

1 Peter 1:17-19

I once spoke at a youth conference where we had a question-and-answer session each night. One student asked about my thoughts on the topic of abortion. I answered, "I think our culture has lost its awe and wonder at the gift of life." This lack of awe at the creation and work of God is reflected in a lack of awe for the Creator Himself.

I grew up in the coastal state of Oregon, and our family took many trips to the beach. Due to our love of wading, exploring, body surfing, and swimming, my parents taught us one important lesson: a healthy fear of the ocean. There were riptides that could drag us out to sea, rogue waves that could knock us down, and even not-so-friendly sea creatures such as stinging jellyfish that could harm us. We were to enjoy the ocean, but we were to always keep an eye out. We were to never lose our reverence for the ocean's power.

Though the ocean doesn't have near the power of the Creator, it seems much harder to give God the respect He's due. Granted, it's not the same kind of fear of the ocean—a worry that God will knock us down and drag us out (or sting us). However, God is the One who created our universe and every aspect of it. A right understanding of His awesome power should lead us to evaluate our attitude toward Him and our relationship with Him.

God is truly worthy of our reverence. Consider just a few reasons why:

▶ God is the all-powerful Creator whose perfect love saved us from ourselves, and did so with finality.

▶ God's power can overcome our habits and former ways.

▶ God can overcome whatever we think we are enslaved to do.

▶ God can make things new, even in a world full of evil.

These (and other) realities cause me to stand in awe before Him.

> *When do people take the fear of God too seriously or not seriously enough?*
>
> *QUESTION #3*

1 Peter 1:22-25

As Christians, we often fail to take seriously the set-apartness of our love for one another. We'll bring food to the sick or help build a playground for the kids. But the moment we disagree—whether it's over theology or the color of the new church carpet—we make the opposition a target for hostility.

Many times these negative actions and attitudes stem from selfishness rather than a focus on Christ. Nearsighted Christians sometimes treat people as objects to be used. They try to rally others around their way of thinking or do "good works" with the goal of being affirmed.

In contrast, notice Peter's emphasis on a pure heart:

▶ A pure heart doesn't love for the purpose of getting something in return.

▶ A pure heart doesn't love only those who think in the same way.

▶ A pure heart doesn't serve itself before all others.

The Word of God calls us to a higher standard: a genuine, sincere love for one another. This standard of love and obedience to Christ is what others will notice. Our Christ-centered, holy love will set us apart from the world around us. The trials and pains of this life will come and go—eventually coming to an end once and for all. But our love for each other will remain when it's grounded in Christ. That's why we're called to strive for a loving, safe place within the church.

What are the implications of God tying our obedience to Him to our love for others?

QUESTION #4

How can we support each other in living holy lives?

QUESTION #5

LIVE IT OUT

How can our lives point to a powerful, holy God?

▶ **Strive for obedience.** As you read God's Word this week, look for principles and commands you can intentionally obey.

▶ **Check your motives.** Evaluate what motivates you to serve God and others. Do you serve to obey God and glorify Him, or do you serve to be affirmed and appreciated? Repent of any skewed motives and move forward.

▶ **Remember God's Word.** Memorize 1 Peter 1:22 this week. Recite that verse at the beginning of each day as a reminder to love others with a pure heart.

Holy living may not lessen the impulse to blend in or to be part of the crowd. But when all eyes do turn your way, they'll see Jesus. So go ahead—be set apart for His sake.

The Mouth Guard

We were enjoying lunch when my son told me about a volunteer at church. "They told him his services were no longer needed," he said. "Can you believe that? He's been doing that job for 10 years. How do you fire a volunteer?" I was outraged. "And he's so good! Who will replace him?" "That's what's wrong with our church. People just go off and say and do things without knowing what they're doing," I said, taking a sip of my chocolate shake. The more I thought about it, the angrier I got. I began to think of other slights I had heard about and things that needed to be straightened out.

To continue reading "The Mouth Guard" from *Mature Living* magazine, visit *BibleStudiesforLife.com/articles*.

My group's prayer requests

....

....

....

....

....

....

....

....

....

....

My thoughts

1. Ipsos, "Social Media Survey," http://www.ipsosna.com/download/pr.aspx?id=11824 (accessed November 15, 2013).

SESSION 3

ENDURING FAITH

What are your best tips for enduring a long road trip?

QUESTION #1

#BSFLenduring

Trust God in every circumstance.

THE BIBLE MEETS LIFE

Have you heard of the Ironman race? It's a grueling event where participants swim 2.4 miles, bicycle 112 miles, and finish up by running a marathon (26.2 miles)—all in less than 17 hours. Many people describe the race as the ultimate test of physical endurance.

You may never run the Ironman, but you've gone through your own tests of endurance. And you've got more tests coming.

As followers of Christ, difficult situations can test our endurance when it comes to trusting God. Maybe we can trust Him during the first few days after a traumatic experience, such as losing a job. But what if those stressful days stretch out to weeks or months—even a year? It's harder to endure in our trust when we can't see the finish line.

In this session, we'll explore Peter's encouragement to put our trust in God—even through hardship—because He is worthy to be trusted. The apostle gave us a reason to endure and continue to do what is right: because God is good.

WHAT DOES THE BIBLE SAY?

1 Peter 2:13-23 (HCSB)

13 Submit to every human authority because of the Lord, whether to the Emperor as the supreme authority

14 or to governors as those sent out by him to punish those who do what is evil and to praise those who do what is good.

15 For it is God's will that you silence the ignorance of foolish people by doing good.

16 As God's slaves, live as free people, but don't use your freedom as a way to conceal evil.

17 Honor everyone. Love the brotherhood. Fear God. Honor the Emperor.

18 Household slaves, submit with all fear to your masters, not only to the good and gentle but also to the cruel.

19 For it brings favor if, mindful of God's will, someone endures grief from suffering unjustly.

20 For what credit is there if you sin and are punished, and you endure it? But when you do what is good and suffer, if you endure it, this brings favor with God.

21 For you were called to this, because Christ also suffered for you, leaving you an example, so that you should follow in His steps.

22 He did not commit sin, and no deceit was found in His mouth;

23 when He was reviled, He did not revile in return; when He was suffering, He did not threaten but entrusted Himself to the One who judges justly.

Key Words

Submit (v. 13)—A military term indicating subordination to or ranking beneath another. It does not indicate slave but rather the acknowledgment of authority.

Honor (v. 17)—To esteem, respect, value, or treat another with graciousness. Honor expresses value and recognizes others as important and of worth.

IN THIS TEMPLE.
AS IN THE HEARTS OF THE PEOPLE
FOR WHOM HE SAVED THE UNION
THE MEMORY OF ABRAHAM LINCOLN
IS ENSHRINED FOREVER

1 Peter 2:13-17

How do we demonstrate our freedom in Christ? One way is to honor those who have authority over us—including governing authority.

This seems like an odd command, given that Peter was writing to persecuted Christians. Why should these people give honor to a government that violated their freedom of religion? The answer is that showing honor proved they were truly free in Christ—they were free *not* to sin against others. They didn't need to agree with the governing authorities' views or actions. Yet, in their own freedom from the slavery of sin, the early Christians were not enslaved to hateful attitudes, words, or actions toward those authorities with whom they disagreed.

This is a picture of true tolerance.

Christians are not supposed to use their freedom in Christ to tear others down—not even in elections. If we truly trust God to care for our needs, even an unwise ruler cannot harm us in the ultimate sense. So, while citizens of the United States have the freedom to speak their minds, citizens of heaven have the freedom to do good and must avoid the slanderous tongue of the evil one. Wise servants of God are those who trust Him as the protector of freedom, and they will not return to the slavery of fear. We are to continue to do what is right and good as members of God's family.

In our desire to control our reputations and social status, we might be tempted to attack those who insult us. But Peter stated that the way to silence ignorant people is by doing good.

> *How do we submit to and honor leaders we disagree with?*

QUESTION #2

We express faith in such circumstances by continuing to act uprightly. Furthermore, our upright actions are grounded in these confidences:

▶ Confidence that God will bring truth to light.

▶ Confidence that, even if God permits falsehoods to be spoken about us, nothing will change the truth that there is no condemnation in Christ and we belong to Him forever.

AUTHORITY ISSUES

Choose two.	What are the implications of Peter's instructions in verses 13-14 for how you respond to the following areas of authority?
☐ Federal government ☐ Local government ☐ Traffic laws ☐ Copyright laws ☐ Taxes ☐ Other	

1 Peter 2:18-20

We sometimes bring suffering on ourselves through our own thoughts and actions. Other times our suffering comes from the unjust hands of others. Consider Peter's example of slaves. He encouraged them to trust the Lord not just in their daily circumstances, but even under the ruthless rule of cruel masters.

How is it possible to persevere under such hardship? Peter wrote that we can endure when we remain "mindful of God's will."

▶ It's not God's will that there be any evil done under the sun.

▶ God is the righteous Judge, and no act of injustice will go unnoticed by the Lord of heaven.

▶ God is faithful to judge both the righteous and unrighteous.

As Christians, what can we offer to those who are suffering injustice or persecution? We can point them to the only good that is worthy of our trust—we can point them to God. He will require an account for our actions since He is a perfectly good and righteous judge. As the perfectly good God, He always does what is good for humankind.

Remember, God knows firsthand about injustice and persecution. Jesus was cursed, spat on, beaten, and put to death to pay the penalty for our sins. Jesus then defeated death by rising from the grave, demonstrating that we can have hope through faith in Him.

God punishes evil, but He also provides hope for us. He doesn't leave us to face the dire consequences of our sin.

Furthermore, there is hope even in the midst of injustice. God honors the one who has suffered. God doesn't forget His people, nor does He allow evil to ultimately go unanswered. Because we trust in God and know His nature, we are called to act as those who truly believe God is the real Lord and Savior of the universe.

How can we understand and apply God's command to submit in these verses?

QUESTION #3

When have you endured persecution or hostility because of your faith?

QUESTION #4

> "Faith is deliberate confidence in the character of God whose ways you may not understand at the time."
>
> —OSWALD CHAMBERS

1 Peter 2:21-23

We *can* endure hardship without sinning, and our example is Jesus. Peter quoted from Isaiah 53, the prophetic "suffering servant" passage that points to the Messiah. Peter referred to this passage because he wanted us to see that even in the most unjust suffering, Jesus did not sin.

Consequently, when we suffer, we are not to sin.

Someone might say, "Jesus didn't sin because He is God. But I'm only a human!" Yes, Jesus was fully God, but He was also fully human. He chose obedience, and so can we. God knows we will not be perfect in our reaction to unjust suffering, as Jesus was, but Christ's response is our goal and our target. His goodness makes it possible for us to do good, even in the face of great darkness and pain.

So what was Christ's example? **Jesus Christ exemplified perfect trust in the only One who judges justly.** Whether you're dealing with a routine situation, your worst suffering ever, or something in between, God can be trusted because He is good. In fact, it's the hope of God's goodness to us that sustains a forward-moving attitude. It's the reason we can endure—because we really do find something better in God.

Ultimately, God will put an end to all suffering and injustice. He has already shown us that He will do so by defeating death and eliminating the major consequence of sin. God raised Jesus from the dead not only to defeat death, but also to restore all that is good. And when we stand with Christ in His goodness, we will stand forever.

> *What are your best tips for enduring our culture's hostility against Christians?*
>
> QUESTION #5

LIVE IT OUT

What steps can you take to trust God in every circumstance?

▶ **Get educated.** Research your local and regional politicians as preparation for engaging your governing authorities in a way that honors Christ.

▶ **Choose freedom.** To be a Christian is to be set free in Christ. Choose to exercise that freedom by not retaliating when someone wrongs or insults you this week.

▶ **Care for the persecuted church.** Connect with a ministry that serves as an advocate for churches and individuals undergoing persecution. Support that ministry through prayer; consider giving financially, as well.

Never lose sight of the goodness of God. Even in the midst of difficult situations, choose to bring honor and glory to Him before the world by enduring with Him in complete trust.

Traveling Light

The airplane cabin was almost completely quiet, except for the occasional clicking of a flight attendant's heels, responding to a passenger's call for hot tea or a pillow. Night had fallen across the vast expanse of sky somewhere between London and Johannesburg—at whatever point along that trajectory we were. And as my husband, Jerry, finished the last sip from his coffee and leaned back against the headrest, I turned to gaze out the window at the thick, velvety darkness, studded everywhere with tiny sequins of starlight.

To continue reading "Traveling Light" from *HomeLife* magazine, visit *BibleStudiesforLife.com/articles*.

My group's prayer requests

....

....

....

....

....

....

....

....

....

....

....

My thoughts

SESSION 4

READY FAITH

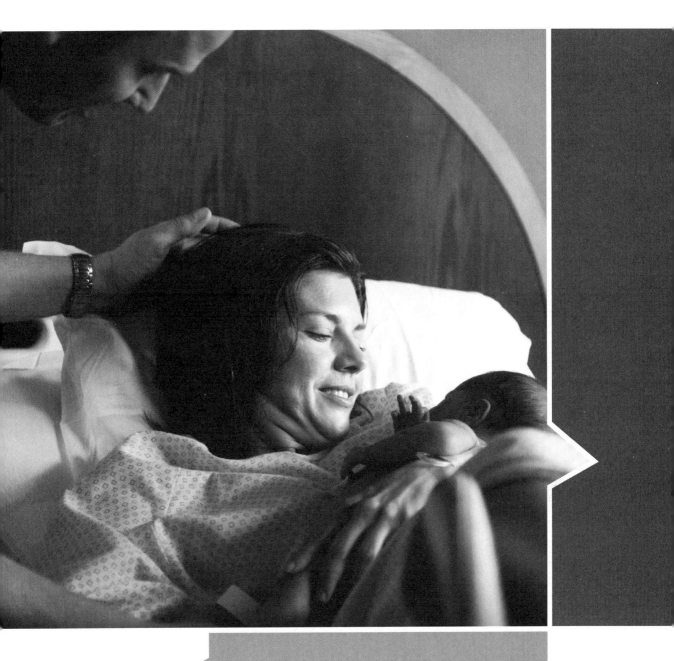

When have you chosen to endure difficulty for a future benefit?

#BSFLready

QUESTION **#1**

Suffering brings opportunities to point to Jesus.

THE BIBLE MEETS LIFE

Beep! Beep! Beep! The alarm goes off before dawn, and you drag yourself out of bed. You get dressed and work your way through a few warm-up exercises, then set off down the road and watch the sunrise while you jog. When you feel like you can't run another step, you push harder so you can make it just a little further than last time.

Why do we do that to ourselves? Why do so many people willingly choose the pain of physical exercise day after day after day? The answer is that we're aiming for a long-term payoff. Specifically, we're working toward a stronger body and better health.

The same principle is true when it comes to enduring suffering as a follower of Christ. No one chooses to suffer for being a Christian; it just comes our way. But we can choose to discover a benefit—an opportunity—that arises out of difficult and painful circumstances.

In the Book of 1 Peter, we discover that a great opportunity comes our way when we stand with Jesus even in the midst of difficulty or persecution.

WHAT DOES THE BIBLE SAY?

1 Peter 3:13-16; 4:1-2 *(HCSB)*

3:13 And who will harm you if you are deeply committed to what is good?

14 But even if you should suffer for righteousness, you are blessed. Do not fear what they fear or be disturbed,

15 but honor the Messiah as Lord in your hearts. Always be ready to give a defense to anyone who asks you for a reason for the hope that is in you.

16 However, do this with gentleness and respect, keeping your conscience clear, so that when you are accused, those who denounce your Christian life will be put to shame.

4:1 Therefore, since Christ suffered in the flesh, equip yourselves also with the same resolve—because the one who suffered in the flesh has finished with sin—

2 in order to live the remaining time in the flesh, no longer for human desires, but for God's will.

Key Words

Suffer (v. 14)—In the New Testament, the Greek term indicates suffering due to righteousness. New Testament writers used it of the suffering of both Jesus and Christians.

Blessed (v. 14)—A state of happiness caused by participation in the kingdom of God and the favor of God upon one's life.

1 Peter 3:13-14

How would you answer Peter's question in verse 13?

QUESTION **#2**

At the time of Jesus' death, Peter was a trembling, fleeing disciple. He was a far different man years later when he wrote the epistle we refer to as 1 Peter. He was willing to suffer persecution and harm in this life because he had come to understand there is more to living than *just* this present life. He was a witness to the resurrection of Jesus Christ, and that event changed everything. It meant that, though he may suffer greatly here on earth, he had a future hope to come—a future in which he would experience the reward of having faithfully trusted God.

I have an apologetics ministry through which I have debated many issues on the subject of the existence of God. I have sometimes been the target of inflammatory reactions and remarks. Some of these attacks I can ignore. Other attacks, however, I have to take more seriously. At one point, I had to ask my family if they were willing to risk the physical harm that could come to any of us because of my ministry. We had to face head-on what we really believed—and what we were willing to sacrifice for that belief.

The same was true of Peter. Over and over again, he had to determine what he really believed:

Why is there a strong connection between suffering and sharing faith?

QUESTION **#3**

▶ When Jesus called on him to step out of the boat and onto the water.

▶ When he was confronted about being a follower of Jesus.

▶ When he experienced the risen Jesus face-to-face.

▶ When he ministered in an area hostile to his faith.

It's time to come to terms with what you actually believe. If this life is all there is—if nothing else exists after this—then it makes sense that we would fear losing life or losing control of any part of it. But a righteous God does exist who knows all things and rightly judges all things. Therefore, your suffering will not escape His notice. He comforts and rewards those who suffer unjustly.

STANDING STRONG

Who in your life has been especially dedicated to standing for his or her beliefs?

What have you learned from his or her example?

1 Peter 3:15-16

Peter commanded believers to be prepared to make a defense for the reason for the hope within us. The word translated "reason" is the Greek term *apologia*, from which we get the English word *apology*. This kind of apology doesn't mean saying you're sorry. Rather, it's the kind of statement lawyers give in court. It's a thoughtful, well-reasoned explanation of a specific conclusion.

As part of his command to honor the Messiah as Lord, Peter included some detailed instructions: be able to give anyone a thoughtful, well-reasoned explanation of why you have hope in Jesus Christ. Since you are making Christ Lord in your life, you should be able to understand—and explain—why you believe He is the Lord.

I had a hard time discussing with people *what* I believed before I understood better *why* I personally believe it. I was intimidated, afraid someone might ask of me an answer for which I was unprepared. My typical way of handling this problem was simply to avoid engaging with people about my belief in God. However, after I began to understand my reasons for believing in God, I became much less intimidated to speak to others.

Peter wrote this command to Christians who might physically suffer for giving a defense of the reason for their hope. The early Christians were faced with the very real possibility of suffering insult and injury for sharing what they believed. Peter encouraged them to use this time as a testimony for their hope in Jesus. What a powerful testimony that would be: to stand in the face of persecution and still provide a reasoned defense for belief in Jesus as the risen Lord!

Peter added a caution to those who make such a defense: do it with gentleness and respect. By doing so, people who condemn or insult you for your beliefs will bring shame upon themselves for how they handled you and your arguments.

> *What does it look like to share the gospel with gentleness, respect, and a clear conscience?*

QUESTION **#4**

1 Peter 4:1-2

Much of my travel involves flying. Recently, I've noticed how easily people get put out by inconveniences: long lines, crowded flights, and so on. Unfortunately, Christians can also feel put out by inconveniences in their church and community. These believers make a spectacle of themselves through grumbling.

In contrast, Peter informs us to "equip" ourselves to suffer as Christ suffered. We should be mentally and spiritually prepared for the kind of suffering that goes far beyond the minor inconveniences of life.

What can you do to prepare yourself for suffering?

1. Become a follower of the One who suffered in the flesh for our sins.

2. Adjust your attitude to match the One who suffered in the flesh. We should expect to suffer, not act put out by every inconvenience.

3. Instead of focusing on your desires rooted in the physical pleasures of this life, focus on living in the freedom you've been given from sin.

As Christians, let's be realistic about our call to suffer. We should expect it. And when suffering happens, whether it is an inconvenience or a time of great trial, the world around us should notice something unusual in our response. **God can use everything that happens in our lives—successes and failures alike—to point others to the salvation and hope found in Jesus alone.**

How do we equip ourselves now to suffer well, as Jesus did?

QUESTION #5

LIVE IT OUT

What steps can you take to live well even in suffering?

▶ **Own your testimony.** Make an apology for your relationship with Jesus Christ. Be ready to share what you believe and why you believe it.

▶ **Study up.** Read a book on Christian apologetics in order to become more familiar with the arguments in support of Christian doctrine and the Christian faith.

▶ **Make a public statement.** Don't believe the falsehood that faith is a private matter. Take a step this week to publicly declare your faith and trust in Jesus Christ.

You've chosen to run the race as a follower of Jesus Christ, which means you've also chosen to experience difficult circumstances. Stay strong. Keep running. And remember to use those difficult circumstances as a way to point to Christ until your race is over.

Love Laid Down

It all happened so fast. At the beginning of 2010, Chad Arnold was a healthy 38-year-old with a wife and two kids. Then the liver condition he'd been living with relatively symptom-free since his early 20s suddenly became more aggressive. He went from swimming laps during his lunch hour several days a week to being told that he needed a liver transplant in order to survive. Mere months later his brother, Ryan, 34, donated 60 percent of his liver to Chad in a fairly routine surgery. Then, four days after surgery, Ryan died from complications, leaving behind a wife and three young children.

To continue reading "Love Laid Down" from *HomeLife* magazine, visit *BibleStudiesforLife.com/articles*.

My group's prayer requests

My thoughts

SESSION 5

JOYFUL FAITH

What turns your good day into a terrible, horrible, no-good, very bad day?

#BSFLjoyful

Choose joy even in life's difficulties.

THE BIBLE MEETS LIFE

Surprises are often nice, and they can sometimes be fun. But then there are those "other" surprises: the routine checkup that turned into, "We need to run some more tests." The pay raise that turned into a pink slip. The church ministry that turned into a church fight.

Sometimes life's surprises are irritating, aggravating, and worse.

Where's the joy in that?

Difficulties, suffering, and persecution may seem like major obstacles to our ability to experience joy, but that doesn't have to be the case. The truth is that suffering and difficulties are going to happen. And although we can never fully prepare for their impact on our lives, we can be certain of God's ability to impart joy to us in the midst of those tough times.

This week's session will help you discover how to experience joy even in life's difficulties. Because you *do* have a choice.

WHAT DOES THE BIBLE SAY?

1 Peter 4:12-19 *(HCSB)*

12 Dear friends, don't be surprised when the fiery ordeal comes among you to test you as if something unusual were happening to you.

13 Instead, rejoice as you share in the sufferings of the Messiah, so that you may also rejoice with great joy at the revelation of His glory.

14 If you are ridiculed for the name of Christ, you are blessed, because the Spirit of glory and of God rests on you.

15 None of you, however, should suffer as a murderer, a thief, an evildoer, or a meddler.

16 But if anyone suffers as a "Christian," he should not be ashamed but should glorify God in having that name.

17 For the time has come for judgment to begin with God's household, and if it begins with us, what will the outcome be for those who disobey the gospel of God?

18 And if a righteous person is saved with difficulty, what will become of the ungodly and the sinner?

19 So those who suffer according to God's will should, while doing what is good, entrust themselves to a faithful Creator.

Key Words

Fiery ordeal (v. 12)—Literally, this references something that was burning. Figuratively it was used here of the trials that purified the readers of 1 Peter.

Christian (v. 16)—Outsiders first used the designation to refer to Jesus' followers as a term of derision rather than as a term of endearment.

1 Peter 4:12-13

Don't be surprised. Rejoice! Peter's words are the very encouragement we need to hear. He wasn't chastising his readers for not trusting God during times of great trial. He reminded them of the truth of God's revelation at the end of times, and he highlighted how that truth should inform their present situations. He wanted them (and us) to gain a more robust perspective on life—to see that something much bigger is going on than what we're currently experiencing.

Peter acknowledged our encounters with suffering, referring to them as a "fiery ordeal." He wasn't glossing over the trouble we experience in this life. Yes, our own fiery ordeals may seem all-consuming. They may ignite with such force that we're tempted to question God's goodness—or even question His very existence. But Peter reminded us that in a world full of evil, we should expect suffering to come upon us, just as it came upon Jesus.

Peter also gave us a couple of ways to respond to suffering:

▶ **Recognize that you are being tested.** We are tested in this life to refine our faith or even to see if we truly possess faith at all. The testing of our faith reveals who we really are, and how we respond to the trial reveals what we really believe.

▶ **Rejoice in following the path of the Lord.** Follow along with this progression: 1) God suffered and sacrificed Himself for all of humanity. 2) You suffer because of your trust in Him. Therefore, 3) You have good reason to believe that your suffering is not in vain.

After Jesus' suffering and sacrifice, God raised Him from the dead. Paul called Him "the firstfruits" (1 Cor. 15:20), which was a reference to the first crops to appear during harvest season. This early crop was a sign—a guarantee—that more crops would follow.

Jesus' resurrection points to the resurrection of all those who follow and worship God. We may suffer with Jesus, but we will also experience glory with Jesus. In this, we can find a way to rejoice in any trial.

> *What does it look like to be joyful even when you don't feel like it?*

QUESTION #2

Complete this report card as a way of evaluating your
recent responses to different tests of faith.

**Demonstrates
confidence in beliefs.**

GRADE: ....

COMMENTS: ....

....

**Able to remain joyful
during trials.**

GRADE: ....

COMMENTS: ....

....

**Willing to endure
persecution.**

GRADE: ....

COMMENTS: ....

....

"Surely what a man does when he is
taken off his guard is the best evidence
for what sort of a man he is."

—C. S. LEWIS

> **When have you been discredited or ridiculed because of your faith?**

QUESTION **#3**

1 Peter 4:14

Over the years of doing apologetics ministry, I've been called a lot of names: hatemonger, bigot, stupid, delusional, dishonest, a "nutter," and much more. (Those are the tame ones!) Most of these come from my interactions on the Internet. However, these are the kinds of insults we can expect as Christians in accordance with Peter's words in verse 14.

Though Peter stated that I'm blessed when I endure slander in the name of Jesus, my typical first response is not, "Wow! I am so blessed." I usually react by reviewing the situation with questions like these: *What did I do? Did I attack or offend the person? Was my original statement or online post motivated by a sin that may have prompted this adverse response?*

These kinds of questions swirl around in my head for a while because I forget that, as one who publicly professes Jesus Christ, I am going to receive insults and ridicule due to the world's hatred toward God. One mention of Jesus in public can be enough to get people uptight or bent-out-of-shape. This is exactly what the apostles experienced when they preached Jesus in public. Paul was even stoned by the people of one city and left for dead (see Acts 14:19).

I offer a caution: some Christians bring slander and insult upon themselves because of their ungodly behavior. In such cases, it's inappropriate to claim that one is "suffering for Jesus." As we saw in 1 Peter 3:16, we are to witness to the truth of Jesus "with gentleness and respect" so that we will not bring shame to the name of our Lord.

Peter reasoned that "you are blessed" when slandered for "the name of Christ," because the Spirit of God is on you. Because the Spirit indwells believers, the Lord Himself will comfort you. **The Holy Spirit rests on you, refreshing and strengthening you to carry on.**

1 Peter 4:15-19

Peter mentioned several obvious activities we should avoid as Christians—murder, theft, evildoing. But he also mentioned a more subtle sin: meddling or being a busybody. Christians should avoid meddling in everybody else's business. When we engage in this kind of behavior, we have nobody to blame but ourselves for any suffering we experience afterward.

There are other times, however, when we need to step up on important issues—such as defending what we believe. This isn't meddling when it's done with gentleness and respect. Instead, defending our beliefs is necessary in light of all the misinformation being spread about Christianity in today's culture.

In verse 19, Peter reminded us to continue to do what is good, even while suffering. Why? Because God is our faithful Creator.

▶ God does not leave us stranded here to endure oppression, suffering, and evil on our own.

▶ God will judge evil for what it is.

▶ God will set things right and back to the goodness He intended at the beginning of creation.

God has shown us His faithfulness through Jesus Christ's life, death, and resurrection. And He will continue to show us His faithfulness through the resurrection and redemption we will fully realize and experience in the end.

Do you struggle with meddlers and murderers being on the same list? Explain.

QUESTION **#4**

In light of these verses, how do we choose joy?

QUESTION **#5**

LIVE IT OUT

What steps can you take to discover joy in all seasons of life?

▶ **Seek joy.** Do something this week that you know will help you experience joy. Don't feel guilty about it, either. Accept your joy as a gift from God.

▶ **Have honest conversations.** Ask your friends and family members if there are areas in which you've caused your own suffering. Listen to what they say, then respond appropriately.

▶ **Trust God.** Read Psalm 71:1-8 several times during a quiet moment this week. Rewrite those verses to express your own requests to God in connection with your current suffering.

Choose to stick with God even when you feel like your heart is breaking or the world is crashing down. That choice will help you grow nearer to Him and begin to understand how He ministers to His children in this world—and that's always a pleasant surprise.

Cookies

One morning many years ago was a springboard to a little miracle in my life, proving beyond a doubt God does indeed provide for our needs — and in such interesting, out-of-the-ordinary ways. In the early 1980s, our country was in the middle of a financial downturn that left many farmers bankrupt and forced even more people into unemployment lines. My husband saw it coming, so we kept adding to a savings account. I believe God gave him wisdom and insight concerning this. Then, just as he predicted, his company closed the doors, and he joined the unemployment lines.

To continue reading "Cookies" from *Mature Living* magazine, visit *BibleStudiesforLife.com/articles*.

My group's prayer requests

My thoughts

SESSION 6

VICTORIOUS FAITH

When was the last time you had to "just grin and bear it"?

#BSFLvictorious

God will strengthen and restore me.

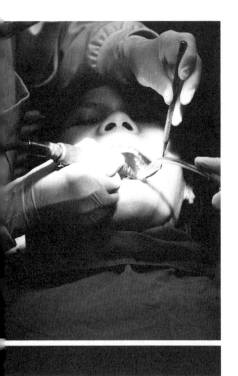

THE BIBLE MEETS LIFE

"Just grin and bear it." "Roll with the punches." "When the going gets tough, the tough get going." When you're feeling down and could use some encouragement, clichés are probably the last thing you want to hear.

The worst is when someone decides to merge two sage phrases into one. Something like: "Just bite the bullet and weather the storm." Is that really the best we can do when someone is hurting?

Many people like clichés and easy answers because they don't require much effort. But when you're on the receiving end, such "advice" feels trite. Most of us are grappling with questions that go much deeper: "Will this ever end?" "Is a greater purpose behind what I'm experiencing?" "Where is God in all this?"

In the Book of 1 Peter, the apostle didn't give us any "easy bake" answers. Instead, Peter offered us a fuller perspective—he showed us a way to deal with our difficulties that goes far beyond "just grin and bear it."

WHAT DOES THE BIBLE SAY?

1 Peter 5:6-11 *(HCSB)*

6 Humble yourselves, therefore, under the mighty hand of God, so that He may exalt you at the proper time,

7 casting all your care on Him, because He cares about you.

8 Be serious! Be alert! Your adversary the Devil is prowling around like a roaring lion, looking for anyone he can devour.

9 Resist him and be firm in the faith, knowing that the same sufferings are being experienced by your fellow believers throughout the world.

10 Now the God of all grace, who called you to His eternal glory in Christ Jesus, will personally restore, establish, strengthen, and support you after you have suffered a little.

11 The dominion belongs to Him forever. Amen.

Key Word

Exalt (v. 6)—Literally means to lift up or to place in prominence. Metaphorically means to esteem or acclaim.

1 Peter 5:6-7

What's the danger of trying to handle life on your own?

QUESTION **#2**

I tend to get worked up over situations I'm trying to handle myself. I'm a perfectionist, which means:

▸ I tend to quit before I even get started because I worry about the end result.

▸ I won't ask for help, because nobody does it like I can.

▸ I know I won't be able to do it perfectly, so I don't do anything at all.

Those excuses may sound like worry, but they're really a form of pride. When we worry, we are trying to fix things ourselves. We don't trust the sovereign Creator God to deal rightly with our situation. That sounds silly when we think about it. I profess a God who can create the universe, who died on the cross for my sins, and who rose from the dead to redeem me and the whole of His creation—yet I still hesitate to trust Him. If ever a person were worthy of my trust, it certainly is God. Yet, my pride gets in the way.

What does it mean— and not mean—to humble yourself?

QUESTION **#3**

Verse 6 calls me to humble myself and allow God to exalt me in the proper time. God is the only One who can rightly raise me up. Why? Because He is perfect in all His ways—even in His dealing with me. If God were not perfect, He would not be worthy of my worship. But He is perfect, and He will rightly deal with all things in His perfect time.

Peter's words in verse 7 give us great encouragement. They remind us we're not insignificant specks in a vast universe. **Remember: the Creator God cares for you right now, wherever you are in life.** God invites you to throw everything on Him and trust the Perfect Caregiver to care for you.

> *"Be serious! Be alert! Your adversary the Devil is prowling around like a roaring lion, looking for anyone he can devour."*
>
> —1 PETER 5:8

1 Peter 5:8-9

A friend of mine, Neil, shared with me a personal story of suffering. He and his wife, Anna, lost their baby girl only nine days after she was born. A darkness came on Anna that she described as the deepest abyss she'd ever known. She didn't know how to move on. Neil began to gently remind her of the truths they had studied together about God and the reality of this world. One of those truths was that suffering was not unique to them. People all over the world experience the pain of death.

Eventually, Anna recognized that death, suffering, and pain will come to everyone. She began to have great compassion for those in her church who were suffering from all sorts of evils: child abuse, chronic pain, cancer, and more.

Anna's compassion for the suffering of others helped her to move through her own time of grief. She realized, as Peter wrote, that our suffering is a fellowship that all believers share across the world—it's not exclusive to us individually. Anna also found that, as she suffered, it helped to remind herself of the truths she had already learned. As Peter stated: "Be serious! Be alert!"

You need to have a sound mind that is ready for action. In order to handle the attacks of the Evil One who seeks to devour you, develop self control that focuses on the truths of God. The Evil One is not going to leave you alone because you are vulnerable; in fact, that's when he's most likely to attack! So, put vulnerability at bay by remaining focused and alert.

Peter tells us what to do to resist the Devil: stand firm in the faith. Know what you believe and why you believe it. Continue to learn about God and the truths He has revealed to us, and stand on these truths of the faith. Knowing your beliefs will help you apply them when you need to stand firm against an attack.

> **The Devil is your adversary. How can this knowledge affect the way you live?**

QUESTION #4

1 Peter 5:10-11

Throughout the Book of 1 Peter, we've been exploring the foundation for real and sure hope that God provides through Jesus—hope for this life and the life to come. Jesus is the example of what awaits us in the resurrection. We will be restored as He was restored. The whole of creation will be made well and whole again because Jesus makes all things new. Something better is coming!

Peter reminds us that, though we may be suffering—and may even suffer to the point of death—we have genuine hope in the reality of an eternal Creator. God is worthy of our trust because of who He is and what He has done. God is the possessor and giver of all grace. He has demonstrated His immeasurable grace by taking on the consequences of evil and death, and defeating it through the resurrection of Christ. This victory and hope is for each of us.

1. God is our foundation for a sure hope.

2. God is the only One worthy of our trust and reverence.

3. God is the reason we can endure suffering and trials with resilient faith.

4. God is victorious.

I'm so thankful for a God who, in His righteousness, provides salvation for humanity. But He added a personal touch as well. Look at the powerful words Peter uses to convey God's love for us: "who called *you* to His eternal glory in Christ Jesus." God will personally restore, establish, strengthen, and support *you!*

God has given me real hope. It's not a delusion. It's not just something I say to make myself feel better. It's a real hope based in the resurrection. It's a hope that I can access and use right now as I endure trials in this life. I can put my trust in Jesus because He is worthy of my trust. My faith is not in vain. There is something better to come. Amen. Come, Lord Jesus!

> *How do we manage the tension of longing for restoration while we suffer in the present?*

QUESTION #5

A PROMISE FOR ALL SEASONS

Record how God's promise of strength and restoration connects with the different seasons of your life.

PAST
When has God strengthened and restored you?

PRESENT
Where do you need strength and restoration now?

FUTURE
What do you anticipate most about your future strength and restoration in eternity?

LIVE IT OUT

How will you approach God for strength and restoration?

▶ **Don't worry.** Be conscious of moments when you experience worry this week. Use these moments as opportunities to express your trust in God.

▶ **Be prepared.** Make a plan for dealing with attacks when they come your way. Identify an area of your life in which you feel vulnerable, then focus on a truth from Scripture that will help you stand strong.

▶ **Plan a retreat.** Take some time in the near future to get away from your daily routine and spend a significant portion of time with God—and only with God.

When you need help, don't worry about how to "let go and let God" or any other catchy phrase. Simply remember that God is the only sure place to ground your hope, and seek Him for your next step.

A Parent's Dilemma

The phone rings. You listen with anguish to the pain in your daughter's voice as she tells of a heartbreaking event in her life. It's all you can do not to rush to her side and do something, anything to ease her pain. As parents, the desire to rescue our offspring never seems to end. When they were little, it was our job to rescue them when they were in trouble. We rushed to soothe their hurts, to make the problem all better. But once they become adults, the line between helping and rescuing is more distinct and more critical.

To continue reading "A Parent's Dilemma" from *Mature Living* magazine, visit *BibleStudiesforLife.com/articles*.

My group's prayer requests

My thoughts

Resilient Faith: Standing Strong in the Midst of Suffering

We have spent the last six weeks in the Book of 1 Peter, discovering truth about faith in God which spurs us onward to live truly free in Christ through the hope of His resurrection—no matter what comes our way. We may be stretched, but we can rely on our resilient faith.

Christt

A resilient faith is one that is grounded in the person and work of Christ. Faith in anything else will prove unreliable. Jesus provides us the example of how we stand resolutely with God regardless of what difficulties or opposition we face.

Community

Believers stand strong when they stand together. Believers can encourage each other through their words and personal experiences.

Culture

The American culture is becoming increasingly hostile toward Christians. We do not need to cower before such opposition; instead, we can stand firm, expressing a love and hope that they cannot explain away. We are called to be holy, set apart from the culture and world's standards around us.

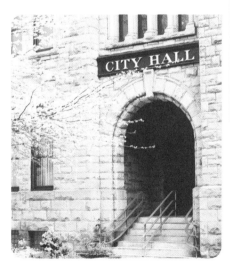

LEADER GUIDE | RESILIENT FAITH

GENERAL INSTRUCTIONS

In order to make the most of this study and to ensure a richer group experience, it's recommended that all group participants read through the teaching and discussion content in full before each group meeting. As a leader, it is also a good idea for you to be familiar with this content and prepared to summarize it for your group members as you move through the material each week.

Each session of the Bible study is made up of three sections:

1. THE BIBLE MEETS LIFE.

An introduction to the theme of the session and its connection to everyday life, along with a brief overview of the primary Scripture text. This section also includes an icebreaker question or activity.

2. WHAT DOES THE BIBLE SAY?

This comprises the bulk of each session and includes the primary Scripture text along with explanations for key words and ideas within that text. This section also includes most of the content designed to produce and maintain discussion within the group.

3. LIVE IT OUT.

The final section focuses on application, using bulleted summary statements to answer the question, *So what?* As the leader, be prepared to challenge the group to apply what they learned during the discussion by transforming it into action throughout the week.

For group leaders, the *Resilient Faith* Leader Guide contains several features and tools designed to help you lead participants through the material provided.

QUESTION 1—ICEBREAKER

These opening questions and/or activities are designed to help participants transition into the study and begin engaging the primary themes to be discussed. Be sure everyone has a chance to speak, but maintain a low-pressure environment.

DISCUSSION QUESTIONS

Each "What Does the Bible Say?" section features at least four questions designed to spark discussion and interaction within your group. These questions encourage critical thinking, so be sure to allow a period of silence for participants to process the question and form an answer.

The *Resilient Faith* Leader Guide also contains follow-up questions and optional activities that may be helpful to your group, if time permits.

DVD CONTENT

Each video features Philip Nation interviewing Mary Jo Sharp about the primary themes found in the session. We recommend that you show this video in one of three places: (1) At the beginning of group time, (2) After the icebreaker, or (3) After a quick review and/or summary of "What Does the Bible Say?" A video summary is included as well. You may choose to use this summary as background preparation to help you guide the group.

The Leader Guide contains additional questions to help unpack the video and transition into the discussion. For a digital Leader Guide with commentary, see the "Leader Tools" folder on the DVD-ROM in your Leader Kit.

SESSION ONE: FOCUSED FAITH

The Point: Our faith is focused on a sure hope.

The Passage: 1 Peter 1:3-9,13

The Setting: Peter wrote this letter to believers scattered across Asia Minor, most of whom were probably Gentile converts. Though Christianity was not officially illegal at the time, many of the letter's recipients likely experienced, or knew the potential for, local persecution and discrimination. Realizing these believers' circumstances, Peter wrote to encourage them to remain strong in their faith, even in the midst of the present difficulties.

QUESTION 1: What situations tend to rattle you?

> *Optional activity:* Pass out a toy magnifying glass to each participant. (Note: these can be found at dollar stores or hobby stores.) Encourage group members to carry the magnifying glass in their purse or pocket throughout the next week as a reminder that our faith is focused on a sure hope.

Video Summary: This video message serves as an overview and background for the entire *Resilient Faith* study. With 1 Peter as the scriptural basis, Philip and Mary Jo begin by talking about Peter and what he has to teach us about faith. Peter makes a case in these verses for faith and belief in God. Peter suffered much persecution as he tried to spread his message in an area that was hostile toward God. He wasn't a religious leader of the day; he was a "common guy." He trusts in God but then at times he doubts. He walked with Jesus, but even so, he experienced the same feelings and emotions we experience today. First Peter lays a foundation for the one thing that is vital to having a resilient faith—a hope in Jesus Christ and His resurrection.

WATCH THE DVD SEGMENT FOR SESSION 1, THEN USE THE FOLLOWING QUESTIONS AND DISCUSSION POINTS TO TRANSITION INTO THE STUDY.

- Peter starts the first verse of 1 Peter 1 with a word of encouragement to the scattered church, knowing that they might be feeling far from God. When have you most felt like a stranger because of your faith?

- In what ways do you think having a focused faith can provide for us the basis for what is yet to come?

WHAT DOES THE BIBLE SAY?

ASK FOR A VOLUNTEER TO READ ALOUD 1 PETER 1:3-9,13.

Response: What's your initial reaction to these verses?

- What do you like about the text?

- What questions do you have about these verses?

TURN THE GROUP'S ATTENTION TO 1 PETER 1:3-4.

QUESTION 2: In what ways do human expressions of hope compare to the inheritance described in verse 4?

This question asks group members to look beyond the words of this passage to discover applicable truths. Ultimately biblical hope doesn't even compare to human expressions of hope in that the former is imperishable, the latter perishable, and empty.

> *Optional follow-up:* What ideas or images come to mind when you hear the word *hope*?

MOVE TO 1 PETER 1:5-7.

QUESTION 3: How have you seen faith tested and strengthened because of a trial?

This self-revelation question is an opportunity to practice community by sharing stories.

> ***Optional follow-up:*** Share an example of a time when you were able to stay focused on being faithful through a fearful experience.

CONTINUE WITH 1 PETER 1:8-9,13.

QUESTION 4: How have you experienced the connection between faith and joy?

This question asks group members to recall a personal experience. The objective is for each member to understand, through story, the causative relationship between faith and joy.

> ***Optional activity:*** Encourage participants to complete the "What Difference Does It Make?" activity on page 11. Ask volunteers to share one area of life in which hope in Christ can influence their perspective.

QUESTION 5: How can our group reflect hope in a fallen world?

This is about application more than "potential." The end-game is for members to mobilize as a group to reflect hope to the world around them. It is sometimes referred to as being "zip code missionaries."

> ***Optional follow-up:*** What kinds of actions would cause that hope to dim in the eyes of those around us?

Note: The following question does not appear in the group member book. Use it in your group discussion as time allows.

QUESTION 6: What is the next step on your journey toward a deeper experience with faith and hope?

This question personalizes the sentiment found in the prior question. As a leader you will want to point out that these answers are only the "first steps" in a larger plan of action.

LIVE IT OUT

Invite group members to consider these three ways they can respond to the reality of a sure hope:

- **Trust in the small things.** Seek out situations in which you can consciously and intentionally express your trust in God each day.
- **Prepare your mind.** Move your focus beyond the material world by reading a book or listening to a sermon series that solidifies your understanding of basic Christian doctrines.
- **Proclaim the gospel.** When you encounter someone who has lost hope, choose to share the good news of Jesus' resurrection and your sure hope for eternal life with Him.

Challenge: The way we think about hope influences the way we think about faith. It's our ability to hope for something better and bigger than our current situation that enables us to act in faith. Spend some time this week considering how you have typically thought of hope and how you can be more deliberate in living your life so that your hope is seen in your steadfast faith in Christ.

Pray: Ask for prayer requests and ask group members to pray for the different requests as intercessors. As the leader, close this time with a prayer of praise. Proclaim your faith in the living hope made possible through the resurrection of Jesus Christ.

SESSION TWO: ACTIVE FAITH

The Point: Live a life that is set apart for God.

The Passage: 1 Peter 1:14-19,22-25

The Setting: Peter sought to encourage first-century believers undergoing persecution by emphasizing to them their call to holiness. They had been set apart from the lifestyles of those around them to live as reflections of a holy God. Though their lives of obedience might initiate or increase persecution, Peter reminded these brothers and sisters in the Lord that this earthly life would quickly fade, but God's call for holiness would endure forever.

QUESTION 1: What are some things the average person considers holy or sacred?

> *Optional activity:* Pass out a magazine or section of newspaper pages to each person in the group. Ask participants to identify advertisements or other content that encourages people to "fit in." As time allows, encourage volunteers to share their findings with the group. Conclude by drawing their attention back to the reality that as Christians we are called to live lives that are set apart for God. Be sure to use magazines and newspaper pages that don't contain offensive or inappropriate material.

Video Summary: This week's video message focuses on how our faith can continue to move forward despite the reality that the world is hard. How do we live differently in the midst of suffering and not be conformed to the world's desires? First Peter 1:14-19,22-25 delivers a call for us to do just that. It is a call to be actively obedient even when we don't know what the outcome will be. Life can feel like it's spinning out of control, but Scripture is a place of permanence to guide us to what is good and true. It is unchanging. It is a platform from which we can live our lives.

WATCH THE DVD SEGMENT FOR SESSION 2, THEN USE THE FOLLOWING QUESTIONS AND DISCUSSION POINTS TO TRANSITION INTO THE STUDY.

- When faced with a trial in your life, how do you most often respond?
- Think of a time in your life when it felt like things were spinning out of control. What were you able to find during that time that felt permanent and unchanging? Explain.

WHAT DOES THE BIBLE SAY?

ASK FOR A VOLUNTEER TO READ ALOUD 1 PETER 1:14-19,22-25.

Response: What's your initial reaction to these verses?

- What questions do you have about these verses?
- What application do you hope to gain about what it means to be holy—set apart—because Jesus is holy?

TURN THE GROUP'S ATTENTION TO 1 PETER 1:14-16.

QUESTION 2: What is your reaction to the commands in verses 15-16?

In asking for a reaction to the text this question establishes the centrality of Scripture for the group. Because honesty and authenticity are important in life, encourage the group to be transparent. "Being holy" can be an overwhelming proposition.

Optional activity: Encourage group members to complete the "What Is Holiness?" activity on page 19. Ask for volunteers to share which image they chose and to explain how that image illustrates their understanding of holiness.

MOVE TO 1 PETER 1:17-19.

QUESTION 3: When do people take the fear of God too seriously or not seriously enough?

Many people operate between two extremes of taking "fear" too literally or not taking the "fear of God" seriously enough. Life experiences, family systems, and interpretation all play a part. This question provides a context for a discussion on how the group might interpret the "fear of God."

Optional follow-up: What are the usual consequences of taking the fear of God too seriously and not seriously enough?

CONTINUE WITH 1 PETER 1:22-25.

QUESTION 4: What are the implications of God tying our obedience to Him to our love for others?

This question is crafted to bring out different attitudes about love and the many relationships each group member has. In extreme cases we have seen obedience manifested as being relationally cold when obedience to God should instead lead to a higher level of love for others. Answering this question requires members to examine the fruit of their obedience and purity of heart.

Optional follow-up: What are some practical ways we can express love to other people within our spheres of influence?

QUESTION 5: How can we support each other in living holy lives?

Be willing to camp out on this question long enough to allow the discussion to develop. In order for group members to support each other in this way, they also have to be willing to be transparent enough to name the ways they can be supported themselves.

Optional follow-up: What are some specific things you can do to grow holiness in your own life?

Note: The following question does not appear in the group member book. Use it in your group discussion as time allows.

QUESTION 6: How can we walk the line between being "set apart" within our community and separating from our community?

While holiness maintains that we are set apart from the world, we are also called to be salt and light. Discuss where those lines are and how they can be navigated. Be willing to manage the tension inherent in this question.

LIVE IT OUT

Direct group member to consider these three ways their lives can point to a powerful, holy God:

- **Strive for obedience.** As you read God's Word this week, look for principles and commands you can intentionally obey.

- **Check your motives.** Evaluate what motivates you to serve God and others. Do you serve to obey God and glorify Him, or do you serve to be affirmed and appreciated? Repent of any skewed motives and move forward.

- **Remember God's Word.** Memorize 1 Peter 1:22 this week. Recite that verse at the beginning of each day as a reminder to love others with a pure heart.

Challenge: Try to be more aware this week of times and situations where you tend to want to "fit in." Holy living may not lessen the impulse to blend in or to be part of the crowd, but when you are deliberate about reflecting God's holiness with your life and all eyes do turn your way, they'll see Jesus.

Pray: Ask for prayer requests and ask group members to pray for the different requests as intercessors. As the leader, close this time with a prayer of commitment. Affirm your desire to live in a way that reflects God's holiness, and ask for His help as you and the members of your group seek to do so each day.

SESSION THREE: ENDURING FAITH

The Point: Trust God in every circumstance.

The Passage: 1 Peter 2:13-23

The Setting: Peter urged the first-century Christians facing the hardship of persecution and discrimination for their faith to concentrate on doing good and not evil. He pointed out that this required submitting to and honoring earthly authorities, even those who practiced cruelty toward them. Peter held up Jesus as their example, who Himself endured undeserved persecution by entrusting Himself to God, who judges justly.

QUESTION 1: What are your best tips for enduring a long road trip?

> *Optional activity:* Set up a brief test of endurance within your group. Ask for a volunteer to lift a slightly heavy object (between 5-10 pounds) and hold it so that his or her arm is perpendicular to his or her body. Encourage the volunteer to keep the object lifted up for as long as possible. If time allows, encourage the rest of the group to guess how long the volunteer can keep the object lifted up. Conclude by drawing the group into the message they will encounter in this week's session—we have a reason to endure and continue to do what is right: because God is good.

Video Summary: In 1 Peter 2:13-23 we see a much different set of circumstances than what we encounter in life today but a central message that applies to us all—how people of faith are supposed to operate with their culture. As believers we are called to obey our leaders as much as we can. If it is clearly sin, we are obviously not to support or participate, but at times it is harder for us to discern these situations because our circumstances aren't always as obvious as pagan idolatry. Our faith has to endure in the midst of our cultural context. We are transformed through salvation, but it doesn't stop there. We continue to grow. The reality is that we aren't always going to hit the mark in how we endure through our suffering, but we have a goal—being Christlike. He is the goal, and this life is a process of learning to endure.

WATCH THE DVD SEGMENT FOR SESSION 3, THEN USE THE FOLLOWING QUESTIONS AND DISCUSSION POINTS TO TRANSITION INTO THE STUDY.

- What conditions make it hard for you to submit to authority?

- First Peter 2:21-22 says, "You were called to this, because Christ also suffered for you, leaving you an example, so that you should follow in His steps. He did not commit sin, and no deceit was found in His mouth." In what ways can these verses seem less like an unattainable standard and more like a goal for how we can endure in faith?

WHAT DOES THE BIBLE SAY?

ASK FOR A VOLUNTEER TO READ ALOUD 1 PETER 2:13-23.

Response: What's your initial reaction to these verses?

- What questions do you have about these verses?

- What new application do you hope to get from this passage?

TURN THE GROUP'S ATTENTION TO 1 PETER 2:13-17.

QUESTION 2: How do we submit to and honor leaders we disagree with?

Try to steer this question more to the "how" than the "why." This question is included because it's a pain point for many and needs to be discussed within godly community.

Optional follow-up: What emotions do you experience at the thought of submitting to leaders you disagree with?

Optional activity: Direct group members to complete the "Authority Issues" activity on page 29. Encourage volunteers to share any implications they found interesting.

MOVE TO 1 PETER 2:18-20.

QUESTION 3: How can we understand and apply God's command to submit in these verses?

This question is purely driven by the text and intended to lead to biblical application. Submission at many levels is part of a disciple's journey.

Optional follow-up: How do these commands apply to your life, specifically?

QUESTION 4: When have you endured persecution or hostility because of your faith?

Persecution and hostility in the Bible is many times different from the persecution and hostility experienced by present-day believers. This is an opportunity to talk about the different forms of persecution today as well as appropriate reactions based on 1 Peter 2:18-20.

Optional follow-up: How have you changed as a result of those experiences?

CONTINUE WITH 1 PETER 2:21-23.

QUESTION 5: What are your best tips for enduring our culture's hostility against Christians?

This question is a logical follow-up to the previous question. Be mindful to point members back to the biblical text throughout the discussion.

Optional follow-up based on 1 Peter 2:23: How can we live by Jesus' example when we're persecuted?

Note: The following question does not appear in the group member book. Use it in your group discussion as time allows.

QUESTION 6: What are your best tips for cultivating a deeper trust in God?

This is an opportunity to explore the spiritual disciplines. This list includes but is not limited to: prayer, stewardship, fasting, worship, Scripture memorization, confession, submission, community, and Bible study.

LIVE IT OUT

Direct group members to these three steps they can take to trust God in every circumstance:

- **Get educated.** Research your local and regional politicians as preparation for engaging your governing authorities in a way that honors Christ.

- **Choose freedom.** To be a Christian is to be set free in Christ. Choose to exercise that freedom by not retaliating when someone wrongs or insults you this week.

- **Care for the persecuted church.** Connect with a ministry that serves as an advocate for churches and individuals undergoing persecution. Support that ministry through prayer; consider giving financially, as well.

Challenge: Difficult situations can test our endurance when it comes to trusting God. Maybe we can trust Him during the first few days after a traumatic experience, but what if those stressful days stretch out to weeks or months—even a year? It's harder to endure in our trust when we can't see the finish line. What in your life is requiring endurance right now? Spend some time this week thinking through how you can be intentional in trusting God with every aspect of this situation, no matter how long it lasts.

Pray: Ask for prayer requests and ask group members to pray for the different requests as intercessors. As the leader, conclude with a prayer of praise. Proclaim once again that God is worthy of our trust in all situations.

SESSION FOUR: READY FAITH

The Point: Suffering brings opportunities to point to Jesus.

The Passage: 1 Peter 3:13-16; 4:1-2

The Setting: Christ followers in Asia Minor (modern-day Turkey) faced local persecution for their faith. In the face of this suffering, Peter encouraged these believers by pointing out to them the blessing they would have if indeed they experienced victimization for their righteousness. In fact, Peter encouraged them to be prepared to gently, respectfully defend the hope they had that allowed them to face the persecution with resolve and confidence.

QUESTION 1: When have you chosen to endure difficulty for a future benefit?

Optional activity: To illustrate the concept of suffering, bring a small cooler filled with ice cubes to the group meeting. Challenge group members to each take an ice cube and squeeze it tightly in their hands for as long as they can stand the burn. (Also bring a few towels or paper towels so that group members can dry their hands and clean any melted ice cubes off the floor.)

Note: You can illustrate the concept of suffering for a future benefit by offering a candy bar or other prize for those who continue squeezing the ice cube until it melts.

Video Summary: This week's message focuses on Christians anticipating and dealing with persecution. First Peter 3:15 says, "Always be ready to give a defense to anyone who asks you for a reason for the hope that is in you." Peter calls us to stand up and be set apart. To always be ready to make a case, even in the midst of our suffering. So what does it look like to defend our faith in the midst of suffering with both power and grace? We are called to defend our faith while also maintaining our holiness. Because God is holy we make our case in a way that reflects His character.

WATCH THE DVD SEGMENT FOR SESSION 4, THEN USE THE FOLLOWING QUESTIONS AND DISCUSSION POINTS TO TRANSITION INTO THE STUDY.

- On a scale of 1 to 10, how ready do you feel to make a case for the hope you have in Christ? Explain your response.

- Mary Jo talks about two ways we deliver our message of hope. Obviously we defend our faith and share the hope that is within us verbally. But how might that same message be shared visually?

WHAT DOES THE BIBLE SAY?

ASK FOR A VOLUNTEER TO READ ALOUD 1 PETER 3:13-16; 4:1-2.

Response: What's your initial reaction to these verses?

- What do you like about the text?

- What new application do you hope to receive about how suffering brings us opportunities to point to Jesus?

TURN THE GROUP'S ATTENTION TO 1 PETER 3:13-14.

QUESTION 2: How would you answer Peter's question in verse 13?

This interpretation question asks group members to examine not only their own faith but also what they really believe (e.g.: Do they really believe nothing can harm them? And, if so, how do they interpret this truth and apply it in an everyday context?).

> *Optional follow-up:* What new hope for your suffering do you find in this verse?

QUESTION 3: Why is there a strong connection between suffering and sharing faith?

This is an opportunity for the group to consider the eternal consequences of sharing their faith as opposed to the short-term challenges—whatever they may be. Suffering is a part of the human condition so, in turn, an "eternal" attitude gives meaning to a disciple's suffering. *Faith* means sharing. *Faith* also translates as having little to no fear and trusting God in what He says.

> *Optional follow-up:* What emotions do you experience when you share your faith with another person?

> *Optional activity:* Encourage group members to complete the "Standing Strong" activity on page 39. As time allows, ask for volunteers to share about a person in their lives who has been dedicated to standing for his or her beliefs.

MOVE TO 1 PETER 3:15-16.

QUESTION 4: What does it look like to share the gospel with gentleness, respect, and a clear conscience?

This question asks group members to interpret the biblical text in their own words and for their own lives. *Resilient Faith* has numerous interpretation questions and each one requires group members to look beyond the words for godly principles.

> *Optional follow-up:* What obstacles do you think prevent Christians from demonstrating these traits as they live out their faith?

CONTINUE WITH 1 PETER 4:1-2.

QUESTION 5: How do we equip ourselves now to suffer well, as Jesus did?

This question asks group members to discuss how they will prepare themselves both mentally and spiritually to "suffer well." This is also an opportunity to point to the centrality of Jesus in the life of a disciple. In those instances in which there are nonbelievers in a group, both be sensitive to their presence and extend an invitation to talk more about being a Christian after the group meeting.

> **Optional follow-up:** When have you felt you had a clear understanding of God's will for a specific situation?

Note: The following question does not appear in the group member book. Use it in your group discussion as time allows.

QUESTION 6: What steps can we take as a group to more intentionally point to Jesus?

Note that this question asks about steps you can take as a group, not as individuals or as a collection of individuals.

LIVE IT OUT

Encourage group members to consider these steps for living well even in suffering:

- **Own your testimony.** Make an apology for your relationship with Jesus Christ. Be ready to share what you believe and why you believe it.

- **Study up.** Read a book on Christian apologetics in order to become more familiar with the arguments in support of Christian doctrine and the Christian faith.

- **Make a public statement.** Don't believe the falsehood that faith is a private matter. Take a step this week to publicly declare your faith and trust in Jesus Christ.

Challenge: If you've chosen to run the race as a follower of Jesus Christ, you've also chosen to experience difficult circumstances. Stay strong. Keep running. And spend some time this week thinking about ways you can use those difficult circumstances to consistently point to Christ until your race is over.

Pray: Ask for prayer requests and ask group members to pray for the different requests as intercessors. As the leader, close this time by thanking Jesus for the suffering He endured on our behalf. Ask Him for strength to transform suffering into something positive, just as He did.

SESSION FIVE: JOYFUL FAITH

The Point: Choose joy even in life's difficulties.

The Passage: 1 Peter 4:12-19

The Setting: Many early believers faced local persecution. Rather than allowing such treatment to take them by surprise or to seem unusual to them, Peter emphasized for these Christians that suffering for their faith in Christ presented them an opportunity for rejoicing. It also presented them with reason and opportunity to glorify God that they could bear the name "Christian."

QUESTION 1: What turns your good day into a terrible, horrible, no-good, very bad day?

Optional activity: Help group members connect with the concept of joy by showing a clip from a movie or TV show in which a person experiences a moment of extreme joyfulness. Use the following questions to unpack the concept of joy:

- What ideas or images come to mind when you hear the word *joy*?
- When have you recently felt joyful?

Video Summary: In this video message Philip and Mary Jo discuss how it is possible to maintain a joyous faith even when we walk through trials. Jesus didn't make Himself immune to suffering, and through this we can learn that joy does come in the end. God uses hardship and suffering in order to have a positive influence in our lives. The outcome of suffering for Christians is unique. We learn. We mature. We grow. And in following 1 Peter 4:19, we find a solid hope that we will be able to find joy in the midst of our suffering.

WATCH THE DVD SEGMENT FOR SESSION 5, THEN USE THE FOLLOWING QUESTIONS AND DISCUSSION POINTS TO TRANSITION INTO THE STUDY.

- First Peter 4:12 says, "Don't be surprised when the fiery ordeal comes among you to test you as if something unusual were happening to you." What false assumption does this verse set straight?
- Does God expect us to be glad we suffer? What do you think He means by "rejoice"?

WHAT DOES THE BIBLE SAY?

ASK FOR A VOLUNTEER TO READ ALOUD 1 PETER 4:12-19.

Response: What's your initial reaction to these verses?

- What questions do you have about these verses?
- What new application do you hope to get from this passage?

TURN THE GROUP'S ATTENTION TO 1 PETER 4:12-13.

QUESTION 2: What does it look like to be joyful even when you don't feel like it?

Even though it can come off as a little cliché, being joyful is actually a choice you make. Even in the midst of suffering you can relate to Jesus and practice Christlikeness. This is important because we're all going to encounter trials that lead to suffering. Being joyful in large part depends on what we really believe to be true.

> **Optional activity:** Ask participants to complete the "Test of Faith" activity on page 49. As time allows, encourage volunteers to share their grade and comments from one section of the report card.

MOVE TO 1 PETER 4:14.

QUESTION 3: When have you been discredited or ridiculed because of your faith?

Storytelling is a part of any effective biblical community. This question creates a context or environment for group members to tell their stories as relate to this topic. Encourage everyone to participate.

> **Optional follow-up:** How do you typically respond in such situations?

CONTINUE WITH 1 PETER 4:15-19.

QUESTION 4: Do you struggle with meddlers and murderers being on the same list? Explain.

There is a tendency to "rate" sins as well as sinners when the fact is we all stand in need of the same grace— the grace only Jesus can give. This question is included to surface any kind of hierarchy where sin is regarded.

QUESTION 5: In light of these verses, how do we choose joy?

Choosing joy isn't necessarily easy, but it is a choice nonetheless. Sharing steps or methods for making this choice is a good discussion for any group.

Optional follow-up: How would you summarize the differences between joy and happiness?

Note: The following question does not appear in the group member book. Use it in your group discussion as time allows.

QUESTION 6: What steps can you take now that will empower you to choose joy in future difficulties?

Plainly stated, this question asks group members to be deliberate in putting a plan in place.

Optional follow-up: In what ways have you been able to choose joy in the midst of suffering in the past?

LIVE IT OUT

Encourage group members to consider these steps they can take to discover joy in all seasons of life:

- **Seek joy.** Do something this week that you know will help you experience joy. Don't feel guilty about it, either. Accept your joy as a gift from God.
- **Have honest conversations.** Ask your friends and family members if there are areas in which you've caused your own suffering. Listen to what they say, then respond appropriately.
- **Trust God.** Read Psalm 71:1-8 several times during a quiet moment this week. Rewrite those verses to express your own requests to God in connection with your current suffering.

Challenge: This week make a conscious commitment to stick with God even when you feel like your heart is breaking or the world is crashing down. That choice will help you grow nearer to Him and begin to understand how He ministers to His children in this world.

Pray: Ask for prayer requests and ask group members to pray for the different requests as intercessors. As the leader, close this time by praising God for making it possible to choose joy even in difficult times. Ask for strength to not only endure difficult situations in the weeks to come, but also to reflect the joy of Christ.

SESSION SIX: VICTORIOUS FAITH

The Point: God will strengthen and restore me.

The Passage: 1 Peter 5:6-11

The Setting: As Peter drew to the close of his letter, he knew he could not shepherd each believer through whatever circumstances came. But God had provided elders among the believers. Peter urged these seasoned Christians to shepherd the local believers through the turmoil. Specifically, these Christ followers were to submit themselves to God, cast the cares of persecution upon Him, stay alert to Satan's efforts to destroy their faith, and resist Satan. Anything less would allow persecution to win.

QUESTION 1: When was the last time you had to "just grin and bear it"?

> *Optional activity:* To help participants interact with the point of this session, bring several protein bars to the group meeting—or several small bottles of a sports drink. Distribute one to each group member as you begin talking about how God is ultimately the One who strengthens and restores us.

Video Summary: Society would define victory as winning, being #1, coming in first. But the biblical definition is found in verses like Matthew 22:37: "Love the Lord your God with all your heart, with all your soul, and with all your mind." It is a life centered on Jesus Christ, no matter what the world around us looks like. And a key piece of being able to live out a victorious faith is found in the use of the word "personally" in 1 Peter 5:10: "The God of all grace, who called you to His eternal glory in Christ Jesus, will personally restore, establish, strengthen, and support you after you have suffered a little." God, although the Almighty Creator, is a personal God who sent His Son to provide for us a new life. A victorious life. Even in the midst of suffering.

WATCH THE DVD SEGMENT FOR SESSION 6, THEN USE THE FOLLOWING QUESTIONS AND DISCUSSION POINTS TO TRANSITION INTO THE STUDY.

- Have you typically defined victory in your own life more by society's standards or biblical standards? Explain.

- In what way does the promise in verse 10 encourage you?

WHAT DOES THE BIBLE SAY?

ASK FOR A VOLUNTEER TO READ ALOUD 1 PETER 5:6-11.

Response: What's your initial reaction to these verses?

- What questions do you have about God's provision of strength and restoration?

- What new application do you hope to get from this passage?

TURN THE GROUP'S ATTENTION TO 1 PETER 5:6-7.

QUESTION 2: What's the danger of trying to handle life on your own?

In discussing dangers, group members should become more aware of the power of sincere fellowship with God. You may want to point out not only how we have not been created to live in isolation, but also how futile it is not to take advantage of the strength we have in relationship with Him.

> *Optional follow-up:* Why is it tempting for us to try and handle life on our own?

QUESTION 3: What does it mean—and not mean—to humble yourself?

This question asks group members to interpret what it means to be humble. Being humble doesn't translate as not fighting for justice, but it does involve submission. The best place to wrestle with tensions such as this is in biblical community.

MOVE TO 1 PETER 5:8-9.

QUESTION 4: The Devil is your adversary. How can this knowledge affect the way you live?

We don't have to look very hard to realize we have an adversary—an enemy that stands between us and being the men and women God created us to be. This question is application in nature and asks group members to discuss how the reality of the enemy affects their day-to-day lives.

Optional follow-up: What can we learn from Scripture about the Devil's abilities and goals?

CONTINUE WITH 1 PETER 5:10-11.

QUESTION 5: How do we manage the tension of longing for restoration while we suffer in the present?

Self-revelation questions engage the question, "How am I doing in light of the truth unveiled in this Scripture?" A good discussion-driven Bible study will not usually have very many of these questions, but they are effective for introspection and taking our deepest questions to God.

Optional activity: Direct group members to complete the "A Promise for All Seasons" activity on page 61. If time permits, encourage volunteers to share their thoughts on the ways God's promise of strength and restoration connects with different seasons of life.

Note: The following question does not appear in the group member book. Use it in your group discussion as time allows.

QUESTION 6: In what areas do you need strength or restoration right now?

Encourage the group, again, to be transparent with one another. Authenticity and transparency are the building blocks for redemptive community. Be prepared to lead with your own answer.

Optional follow-up: How does knowing that suffering is temporary help you face today's troubles?

LIVE IT OUT

Invite group members to consider these ways to approach God for strength and restoration:

- **Don't worry.** Be conscious of moments when you experience worry this week. Use these moments as opportunities to express your trust in God.

- **Be prepared.** Make a plan for dealing with attacks when they come your way. Identify an area of your life in which you feel vulnerable, then focus on a truth from Scripture that will help you stand strong.

- **Plan a retreat.** Take some time in the near future to get away from your daily routine and spend a significant portion of time with God—and only with God.

Challenge: Take time this week to think about the clichés you've heard, and maybe even used yourself, related to dealing with difficulties. The Book of 1 Peter doesn't give us any "easy bake" answers. Instead, it offers a fuller perspective—a way to deal with difficulties that goes far beyond "just grin and bear it." Rest in the knowledge that you can replace those tired, pithy answers with real solutions that will weather any storm.

Pray: As the leader, close this final session of *Resilient Faith* in prayer. Ask the Lord to help each of you as you move forward to use the principles you have learned in this study to maintain a resilient faith and stand strong regardless of what comes your way.

Note: If you haven't discussed it earlier, decide as a group whether or not you plan to continue to meet together and, if so, what Bible study options you would like to pursue. Visit *LifeWay.com/smallgroups* for help, or if you would like more studies like this one, visit *biblestudiesforlife.com/smallgroups*.

WHERE THE BIBLE MEETS LIFE

Bible Studies for Life™ will help you know Christ, live in community, and impact the world around you.
If you enjoyed this study, be sure and check out these other available titles.* Six sessions each.

Pressure Points *by Chip Henderson*

When Relationships Collide *by Ron Edmondson*

Do Over: Experience New Life in Christ *by Ben Mandrell*

Honest to God: Real Questions People Ask *by Robert Jeffress*

Let Hope In *by Pete Wilson*

Productive: Finding Joy in What We Do *by Ronnie and Nick Floyd*

Connected: My Life in the Church *by Thom S. Rainer*

Resilient Faith: Standing Strong in the Midst of Suffering *by Mary Jo Sharp*

Beyond Belief: Exploring the Character of God *by Freddy Cardoza*

If your group meets regularly, you might consider Bible Studies for Life as an ongoing series. Available
for your entire church—kids, students, and adults—it's a format that will be a more affordable option
over time. And you can jump in anytime. For more information, visit **biblestudiesforlife.com**.

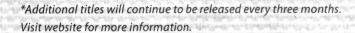

biblestudiesforlife.com/smallgroups
800.458.2772 | LifeWay Christian Stores

Additional titles will continue to be released every three months.
Visit website for more information.